ideals®
COUNTRY ROADS

There is orange down in the valley;
I see crimson 'long the lane.
Yellow spreads across the mountain —
Now that autumn's here again.
There is nothing so enthralling
As a mid-October ride
To see the Master Artist's work
Enflame the countryside.

Earle J. Grant

ISBN 0-8249-1037-0 350

Publisher, Patricia A. Pingry
Editor/Ideals, Dorothy L. Gibbs
Managing Editor, Marybeth Owens
Photographic Editor, Gerald Koser
Research Editor, Linda Robinson
Editorial Assistant, Carmen Johnson
Editorial Assistant, Amanda Barrickman
Phototypesetter, Kim Kaczanowski
Art Director, Patrick McRae

IDEALS — Vol. 42, No. 6 August MCMLXXXV IDEALS (ISSN 0019-137X) is published eight times a year,
February, March, May, June, August, September, November, December
by IDEALS PUBLISHING CORPORATION, Nelson Place at Elm Hill Pike, Nashville, Tenn. 37214
Second class postage paid at Nashville, Tennessee and additional mailing offices.
Copyright © MCMLXXXV by IDEALS PUBLISHING CORPORATION.
POSTMASTER: Send address changes to Ideals, Post Office Box 148000, Nashville, Tenn. 37214
All rights reserved. Title IDEALS registered U.S. Patent Office.
Published simultaneously in Canada.

SINGLE ISSUE — $3.50
ONE YEAR SUBSCRIPTION — eight consecutive issues as published — $15.95
TWO YEAR SUBSCRIPTION — sixteen consecutive issues as published — $27.95
Outside U.S.A., add $4.00 per subscription year for postage and handling

Front and Back Covers
TREE-LINED COUNTRY LANE
Fred Dole

A Vagabond Song

There is something in the autumn that is native to my blood —
Touch of manner, hint of mood;
And my heart is like a rhyme,
With the yellow and the purple and the crimson
   keeping time.

The scarlet of the maples can shake me like a cry
Of bugles going by.
And my lonely spirit thrills
To see the frosty asters like a smoke upon the hills.

There is something in October sets the gypsy blood astir;
We must rise and follow her,
When from every hill of flame
She calls and calls each vagabond by name.

Bliss Carman

The Country Road

There is a winding country road
With memories all the way
From the one-room school to the meadow —
Loved scenes of yesterday.

The meadow I remember best;
I hear the same birds call
And see the black-eyed Susans
That welcomed one and all.

Beside that winding country road,
Near fields of harvest corn,
I see the old farm homestead,
The place where I was born.

And flowing by is Indian Creek
With legends old and sweet.
Its murmur seems to softly say,
"Here time and old friends meet."

Each autumn, it is good to go
Down that winding country way;
For it's the memory link that binds
Today with yesterday.

Mamie Ozburn Odum

CEDAR GROVE 13
HALES CORNERS 27
BIG BEND 8

The Leisure Road

I like the less-used leisure road,
The common little country road
  Far from a city street;
The never-in-a-hurry road,
The have-the-time-to-loiter road
  For easy-ramblin' feet;
The dry, meandering desert road,
The blooming cactus-bordered road
  Where whirling winds compete.

I like the lonely waif-like road,
The shy, retiring, backward road
  That fields of daisies greet;
The grass-grown, long-forgotten road,
Neglected, muddy pasture road
  That hears the lamb-babe's bleat;
The rocky, rough, and rutted road,
The hard-to-find, lost-hermit road
  That into woods retreats.

I like the mountain-climbing road,
The daring winding-upward road
  Where pines and aspens meet;
The turning, twisting, curving road,
The cleaving, clutching, clinging road
  No mountain can defeat.
I like the old return-home road,
The flaming-trees-of-autumn road
  With memories replete.

Myrtle Van Campen

CEDAR GROVE 13
HALES CORNERS 27
BIG BEND 8

Overleaf
CABIN ON THE ROAD
Strafford, VT
Gene Ahrens

The Ole Rail Fence

It was one of those rare days in October. The haze of Indian Summer hung like a shroud over the countryside as if to protect the delicate coloring from the bright glare of a searching sun. The softness of a lingering summer blended with the crisp, cool breeze of twilight that forebode the approach of winter, and all nature had suspended the stern activity of production and was busy preening herself in gorgeous array for a grand finale.

A feeling of peace and contentment seemed to envelop the entire world; a feeling that was somewhat tinged with sadness upon the realization that such serene beauty and hypnotic grandeur was the last lingering gesture of nature in all her intricate finery saying farewell to the verdant days of summer before assuming the bleak role of nakedness for the coming winter. But, fascinated by her alluring artistry, I was led on and on through lanes of gold and scarlet and amber to the next hilltop, there to descend along avenues of amethyst to the little valley below where a leaf-laden brook wound feebly along its way between banks fringed with fading green.

As I reached the crest of the highest hill for one last look, a setting sun added its crowning touch of glory to the resplendent blend of color that cascaded from the hilltops to the valley below, where my gaze became focused upon a little log cabin all but smothered in a blaze of beauty. This little rustic American home, wrapt in a blanket of tranquility and apparently at peace with the world, seemed to symbolize the happiness and quietude for which many strive but few attain.

An air of domesticity hovered about the premises. A motley breed of chickens wandered aimlessly about the yard. A friendly-looking dog made his way lazily out to the leaning old barn and entered through an opening left by a slanting door carelessly hung on one hinge. An old man in shirt-sleeves and vest, staring intently at nothing in particular, leaned nonchalantly against a tree and in a chair of dubious structure. And surrounding this peaceful little scene, with the dead red of bittersweet hanging in clusters from its corners, ran an old rail fence, as though to proclaim to the world that it held at least *this* much of the earth in peaceful recluse.

Ray Whyte

Step Softly Here

Step softly here,
   The daisies sleep,
Across their petals
   Rust stains creep.

Bright leaves that caught
   The fire and gold
Of summer's sun
   Now loose their hold.

Step softly here,
   Where herons cry,
Where wild geese form
   A wedge in the sky.

Disturb no dream,
   No cricket's strum;
Step softly here,
   Lest winter come.

Emily Carey Alleman

Photo opposite
NATIVE LEAVES
Jeff Gnass

Country Chronicle

On foot or by car, a country man will follow the country roads that wind uphill and down, through meadows, fields, and woodlands, across wild pastures, down orchard rows, and over brooks and singing streams fed by springs far up the tree-covered slopes. The experience gives him a more intimate association with the land.

The man's love for those roads dates back to earlier years when an old dirt road curved down the hill and past his house before starting its climb up the long grade on the opposite side of the valley. It was an inviting lane accustomed to the footprints of the team, the iron rims of wagon wheels, and the runners of sleighs.

As a boy, he walked this way to the little one-room school. Walking the mile each way tuned his ears to bird songs and opened his eyes to blossoms unfolding their ribbons of beauty over the meadow and along the roadside. He was witness to the changing seasons.

He still prefers walking to riding. It gives him leisure to listen to the melodies of the woods and fields. It gives him time to look out over the spreading acres to take note of the good husbandry of the farmers who live along the road.

There is an abundance of wild flowers: Queen Anne's lace with its intricate blooms, wild morning glories twining up and over a tangled mass of honeysuckle vines, asters parading across the hills. Passing among them, a man has time to admire, to meditate, and to dream — he has time for reflection.

Summer is gone. The fields no longer simmer under the blazing heat of the sun's shimmering waves. Autumn is the next chapter in the book of seasons to be read slowly and intently so that nothing is lost, nothing left unseen, unheard. A man traveling a country road steps to the rhythm of nature as it edges ever nearer glorious October.

Lansing Christman

October Song

It's showering yellow leaves today,
The lowmost limbs are bare,
And there's a lusty pungency
Like challenge, in the air.

I'll take your challenge, Autumn,
Lay down my years, my load,
To roam like a child in the woodland
And down the river road.

Then when age makes me prisoner
This zest, this tang, shall stay
And set my old lips singing
It's showering leaves today!

Kunigunde Duncan

Photo opposite
WET ROAD
Fred Sieb

ROADS TO TOWN

Those roads to town, please, watch with me
And see them as they used to be,
Made of gravel — dusty, rough,
Yet, for their needs, quite good enough.

Straining teams with heavy loads
Plied those winding, hilly roads.
The wagons groaned o'er clumps of ground —
Their treasured cargo market-bound.

Drivers shouted "Gee!" and "Whoa!"
For their teams to stop or go.
And as the horses thundered by,
Pebbles scattered, earth to sky.

Buggies painted black and red
Passed quietly on rubber tread
Taking lovers for a ride.
By Saturday, she'd be his bride.

Surries, too, with fringe atop,
Bore families to town to shop
And back again, from yonder town,
To be at home 'fore sun was down.

So we've come, and so we've gone —
Year by year, those roads go on,
And we know well, 'neath sun or shade,
Along those roads our lives are made.

George Hugh Baldus

Photo opposite
1923 FORD WAGON
Fred Dole

Wood-Be Roads

Back in the 1800's, travelling on country roads was often a bigger adventure than most people cared for. The roads were awful. The slightest rain could turn a dirt road into sludgy chaos, and many a horse and cart never made its destination. Even in good weather, tree roots and wheel ruts created a bumpy and dangerous obstacle course.

Something had to be done. Among the alternatives were: crushed stone, charcoal, even logs laid side by side, but the charcoal and logs were rejected as inadequate and the crushed stone was just too expensive. Finally, someone, somewhere, thought of using wooden planks. Where wood was plentiful, the price certainly was right.

Russia and Canada were probably the first to build these wooden roads, but America took notice and quickly followed suit. The first American plank road opened in 1846 in New York; its success started a plank road craze that swept the country.

A typical plank road resembled an overgrown sidewalk. Eight-foot planks made from woods like white oak or hemlock were placed across oak "stringers" embedded in the ground. The planks were seldom nailed down because nails could work loose and injure horses or livestock. The road surfaces were slanted to let water run off and trenches were dug alongside to carry away the excess water. But, even with these precautions, water occasionally would get under the road, and some of the planks would float away.

The main advantage of a plank road was that it made travel more efficient. Because its smooth surface reduced wheel friction, horses could pull loads two or three times heavier than before; consequently, farmers made fewer trips to town to sell their goods. Travel was so improved that a trip that once took six days could be completed in three — regardless of the weather.

When plank roads were in their heyday, the state of Wisconsin had one of the biggest networks — the abundance of standing timber made plank roads a natural choice; over 100 roads stretched for nearly 2000 miles over the state. The longest and best remembered was the Watertown Plank Road. Completed in 1853 by the Madison, Watertown and Milwaukee Plank Road Co., it spanned 58 miles between the cities of Milwaukee and Watertown.

Milwaukee desperately needed the road as a way to speed trade to and from the growing city, but construction was slow. During periods of mild weather, people felt that the old road was good enough, so progress on the plank road suffered. Only after fierce spring rains in 1848 crippled the area did enthusiasm for the new road return. Once it was completed, farmers, merchants, and travellers heralded it as "one of the best laid roads in the Union."

In Wisconsin and all over the country, the plank roads stimulated trade, increased the value of adjacent land, and generated plenty of jobs. Travelling sawmills followed the roads as they developed, and eager men awaited expansion into their areas.

The plank roads were built to serve cities. Traffic typically included wagonloads of wheat, barley, flour, wood, and lime. Since imports were so important to the growing cities, the traffic travelling toward town usually had the right of way. Outbound wagons had to do their best on one-lane sections to allow passage, often leaving the road surface entirely. To help a wagon remount, the planks were laid in groups with staggered ends so the wheels would have a projection on which to grab hold.

Photo Courtesy of Milwaukee County Historical Society

A common sight along the plank roads was the toll gate. Tolls — usually one cent a mile per wagon or two cents for a "neat score of cattle" — were collected at five- or ten-mile intervals to help defray the cost of building and maintenance. Building a plank road cost $1000 to $2000 per mile. Initial funding came from common stock sold to public investors. Money for maintenance came from the tolls. Free passage was allowed only to persons attending church services, funerals, or court or military duty. Some users, to avoid paying the toll, travelled in wide circles to get around the toll gates.

In spite of the toll-dodgers, most of the roads managed well enough financially. The Watertown Plank Road, however, was one of the few plank roads to actually make money. Its weekly income often exceeded $1000, and stockholders enjoyed regular and hefty dividends.

Unfortunately, plank roads were not without their drawbacks, the biggest being longevity. Advocates estimated that the life of a wooden road would be ten years. In reality, it was closer to five. Even though the best hardwoods were used, the planks suffered constant damage from weather and high traffic volume. When the sturdier railroads took over, plank roads were destined to fade into obscurity. By 1860, most were neglected and forgotten. Although their place in history was transitory, the role of plank roads in the development of this country's cities had been most vital.

Tom Gill

Roadside Bounty

The autumn harvest lies beside
A road we'll take one crisp, clear day
When fall descends upon our land
And beauty takes our breath away.

The farmer's crop will be displayed
For city folks out for a drive,
And country neighbors — they'll stop, too,
To pick a pumpkin for a pie.

There will be gourds, in orange and green,
And yellow squash, some pale, some bright;
That russet-colored Indian corn
Will hang upon our door at night.

With Nature splashing fruitfulness
In blazing colors o'er the land,
It's easy to feel grateful for
The bounty of a roadside stand.

Amanda Barrickman

Photo opposite
ROADSIDE BOUNTY
Fred Dole

Roadside Rhyme

Remember the roads of the not-too-distant past and those leisurely rides through the country in your roomy DeSoto? Ah, those country roads — those narrow two-laners that jostled us with potholes and slowed us down with hairpin curves and an endless procession of small towns. As we came around a bend, a small town in sight, speed limits dropped from 45 to 35 to 25, even 15 m.p.h. if schoolchildren were around. Then, before we could say "25, 35, 45," we were breezing across the countryside again, sooner or later to be held up behind a tractor pulling a haywagon through a no-passing zone.

All the same, the pace of the country road was pleasant. Remember how the telephone poles whispered to us as we rolled along absorbing all that we could through a car window. And one thing we didn't mind slowing down for was a little roadside rhyme, courtesy of Burma-Shave. For more than three decades, Burma-Shave signs were a welcome source of roadside amusement, as well as a stroke of advertising genius. For those who don't remember them, they were a series of small road signs that unfolded a clever rhyme or a jaunty jingle to advertise shaving cream.

The man behind the signs was Allan Odell of Minneapolis, Minnesota. Exasperated as a travelling salesman, Odell glimpsed his pot of gold at the end of the rainbow on a road between Aurora and Joliet, Illinois. He happened to drive by a set of small signs advertising a nearby gas station and leading him directly to the station's front door. Why not sell shaving cream that way, thought Odell. So, in 1926, with a set of experimental signs lining a highway outside of Minneapolis, he put Burma-Shave on the road to becoming a national brand.

At first the signs were simply advertisements: SHAVE THE MODERN WAY/FINE FOR THE SKIN/DRUGGISTS HAVE IT/BURMA-SHAVE. As the signs became more numerous, they also became more humorous: FOR PAINTING/COWSHED/BARN OR FENCE/THAT SHAVING BRUSH/IS JUST IMMENSE. The rise of competitive brands of shaving cream and the introduction of the electric razor inspired this suggestion: GIVE THE GUY/THE TOE OF YOUR BOOT/WHO TRIES/TO HAND YOU/A SUBSTITUTE

FOR/BURMA-SHAVE. Romantic rhymes played with the allure of a clean-shaven face: HE HAD THE RING/HE HAD THE FLAT/BUT SHE FELT HIS CHIN/AND THAT/WAS THAT.

Public safety messages appeared in 1935: DON'T TAKE A CURVE/AT 60 PER/WE HATE TO LOSE/A CUSTOMER. Clever spoofs prompted many a driver to be more attentive: AT INTERSECTIONS/LOOK EACH WAY/A HARP SOUNDS NICE/BUT IT'S HARD TO PLAY. Some of the public service jingles extended beyond the highway. Smokey Bear must have been pleased with: MANY A FOREST/USED TO STAND/WHERE A/LIGHTED MATCH/GOT OUT OF HAND.

Each rhyme was presented, a line at a time, on four or five signs positioned about 30 yards apart, and each was followed by a final sign bearing the Burma-Shave logo. Such a presentation proved to be very effective advertising; it held the attention of its audience as motorists invariably slowed down to read the verses. Furthermore, the appealing little rhymes replayed themselves in the minds of their readers, much like a favorite song. They provided relief, amusement, and, often, a moment of expectant joy as a youngster awaited his turn to read the next group of signs to fellow passengers.

An endless supply of new jingles was insured by a yearly contest awarding $100 to each writer whose lines were selected for roadside use. Between 1926 and 1963, over 7000 sets of Burma-Shave signs graced the nation. While the size and color of the signs changed from time to time, the humor remained the same:

1930: HALF A POUND/FOR HALF A DOLLAR/AT THE DRUG STORE/SIMPLY HOLLER/BURMA-SHAVE.

1940: HE'S THE BOY/THE GALS FORGOT/HIS LINE/WAS SMOOTH/HIS CHIN WAS NOT

1950: VIOLETS ARE BLUE/ROSES ARE PINK/ON GRAVES/OF THOSE/WHO DRIVE AND DRINK

1960: BEN/MET ANNA/MADE A HIT/NEGLECTED BEARD/BEN-ANNA SPLIT

Although Burma-Shave signs have yielded now to flashier billboards and neon displays, their roadside rhymes live on in the memories of many. As for advertising, no gimmick lasts forever; few have lasted as long. Fortunately, road signs are not the only way to sell shaving cream: OUR FORTUNE/IS YOUR/SHAVEN FACE/IT'S OUR BEST/ADVERTISING SPACE/BURMA-SHAVE.

Kathy Halgren

Old Church Bell

The echo of the old church bell
In our small, country town,
For a hundred years, like leaves adrift,
Has floated softly down.

The echo of the old church bell
Aloft in autumn air
Is a welcome sound we stop to hear
While reaping harvest fare.

The silvery echo of the bell
Sails soft as thistle-down
As it chimes our prayers to heaven
And brings God to our town.

Stella Craft Tremble

Nostalgia

The country road lies so content
Beside the pasture fences;
The sweet fresh scent of new-mown hay
Captivates our senses.

Now further down its sunny way,
Hazy hills are seen,
And a lady in her lace-fenced yard
Looks happy as a queen.

The road glides through a tunnel;
Its sides are big, tall trees,
And its leafy top makes patterned shade
A-flutter in the breeze.

A rippling lake, so clear and blue,
Just down the road a ways,
Invites all passers-by to linger
There these autumn days.

Then, past the lake, the road reveals
More lovely, tree-lined places,
And folks we see along the road
All have such friendly faces.

Even when it rains, this road,
Although 'tis muddy-wet,
Bestows on those who travel it
A peace they can't forget.

A country road beside a fence,
Chain-link, or wood, or stone,
Has special gifts for travelers
And a charm that's all its own!

Verna Smith

Seeds

Little seeds, little seeds,
What power you hold;
Although small in size,
You're worth more than gold.

Blessed with God's sunlight
And rain from His sky,
You bring forth more treasures
Than money could buy.

Emily Scarlett

The Reason for Autumn

Brown-eyed Susans roam the hills;
Purple asters wave their sprays;
Milkweed seeds burst prison pods,
Then ride the wind through autumn days.

Blue-black carrion berries cling
To weathered fence and weathered wall;
Bittersweet orange berries glow —
All have answered autumn's call.

Bertha R. Hudelson

Mildred L. Jarrell

Mildred L. Jarrell was once quoted in her local newspaper as having said, "Oh, I'm in love with autumn." That sentiment, along with the quality of her work, makes Mrs. Jarrell an appropriate choice as this issue's Best-Loved Poet.

Born and raised in Wilmington, Delaware, Mrs. Jarrell later settled in Newark with her husband and son. Her family was her greatest pleasure, and it inspired much of her poetry. She referred to her work as "homespun poetry." That she was inspired also by nature and wildlife is evident in the selection of poems we've chosen here, as well as in the many poems she wrote for children. The subjects of her children's poems were tiny woodland folk and forest creatures. Some of those same little forest animals appeared in her hand-made crewel work.

Although now deceased, Mrs. Jarrell was an Ideals contributor for more than 20 years. She once commented that she felt lucky if Ideals published only a half dozen or so of her poems a year. Perhaps she didn't realize that Ideals was just as lucky to have such a capable and dedicated contributor.

Down a Country Lane

I wander down a country lane
Past meadows cool and sweet,
Where oak and maple lend their shade
And ferns grow at my feet.

The birds sing out a welcome song;
A stream flows quietly,
And sunlight dancing through the trees
Brings memories back to me.

A spider spins a silver web
Among some branches brown.
I shuffle through the fallen leaves
That gather on the ground.

I try to seek, whene'er I can,
A winding lane to roam,
For in the quiet countryside,
My heart is truly home.

A Wooded Path

A wooded path lures my heart along —
Whispering, whispering autumn's song.
Shimmering sunbeams drift through the trees,
Highlighting carpets of russet-gold leaves.

Grey clouds reflect in the murmuring creek;
A windblown leaf has touched my cheek.
I think that autumn is saying goodbye —
You can tell by the breeze; you can see by the sky.

A wooded path calls to my wandering feet;
The crisp smell of autumn is incense sweet.
I've treasured each day of her radiant glow —
Autumn, don't be in a hurry to go.

Fall Fashions

I walked the lanes of autumn
On a bright October day,
And fall displayed her fashions
Of red and gold so gay.

The woodsy scent of autumn,
The haze that cloaks the hills,
The fields adorned with pumpkins —
All are autumn thrills.

I strolled amid the splendor
Of autumn's gifts to man,
And said goodbye to summer
With memories in hand.

Wandering Country Road

A country road meanders far;
It curves around a golden field,
Then reaches toward a meadow high,
And runs beside the daisy yield.

It passes near a woodland stream
Where minnows dart in glinting sun;
It turns toward blue-black shadowed hills,
And, still, its journey's just begun.

Wandering by an old rail fence,
It skirts a cabin in a glade,
Then winds among a stand of pines
Where pungent scents drift in the shade.

Far and away, still rolling on,
This earthen ribbon, banded green,
Has as its aim adventuring,
And jaunts to places yet unseen.

A country road has gypsy feet —
It passes by, but will not stay,
And ever-changing beauty lies
Along its ever-wending way.

Come Along

Come along and walk with me;
We'll wander down the lanes,
Enjoying country sights and sounds
And hearing birds' refrains.

Come along and see the brooks
Tinkling as they go,
Whispering secrets to the banks
Where willows bend down low.

Come along and hear the breeze
Singing through the trees,
While birdlings sleep to lullabies
And woodland melodies.

Come along and greet the sun
That lights the road today.
Come bask in Mother Nature's charms
This lovely autumn day.

Overleaf
WHEATFIELD
Ed Cooper

Farmer's Son

You see him out there raking hay,
Bareheaded, on a sunny day;

Though young in years, so husky, tan,
He's working like a grown-up man.

He knows the tractor inside out;
Was raised up with such things about,

And, ever since he learned to walk,
He's followed Dad, learned tractor talk.

The binder and combine give him joy;
He runs them well, this farmer boy.

His hands are nimble with each tool.
The farm is like a second school

Where he's learning, day by day,
A hundred things that come his way.

He milks the cows and stooks the grain
And dreams his dreams in sun and rain.

His cheery smile makes dark days bright;
He lives what's honest, good, and right

And fills his days with useful toil
About the farm with stock and soil.

He loves his dog, the horses, too,
The pasture trails, the sky so blue —

In peace he sleeps when day is done,
Content to be a farmer's son.

Elma Helgason

Apple Desserts

APPLE-ALMOND TART

1¾ cups flour
¼ cup sugar
½ cup finely chopped almonds
2 teaspoons grated lemon peel
¾ cup unsalted butter, chilled and cut into 1-inch pieces
2 egg yolks mixed with 2 tablespoons cold water
1 teaspoon vanilla
Baking beads *or* dry beans *or* rice
¼ cup unsalted butter, softened

1¾ cups blanched almonds, finely ground
¾ cup sugar
3 tablespoons flour
¼ cup Amaretto liqueur
2 eggs
8 large green apples, peeled, cored, and cut into ¼-inch slices
2 tablespoons unsalted butter
3 tablespoons sugar
½ cup apricot preserves

Crust: In a large bowl, combine flour, sugar, almonds, and lemon peel. Add butter pieces and mix with a pastry blender until the mixture resembles coarse meal. Add egg mixture and vanilla; stir just until blended. Wrap dough in waxed paper and chill for 20 minutes. Roll dough into a 14-inch circle; place in a 10-inch flan tin with a removable bottom. Push dough carefully against sides of tin; cover with parchment paper or foil and press to fit sides. Distribute baking beads, beans, or rice evenly over center of paper to weight it down. Bake at 375° for 10 minutes. Remove paper and baking beads.

Filling: In a food processor, mix softened butter with almonds, sugar, and flour. Add Amaretto and eggs; mix just until blended. Spread mixture evenly over crust. Arrange apple slices in overlapping concentric circles on top of the almond filling. Dot apples with butter and sprinkle with sugar. Bake tart at 375° for 45 to 60 minutes or until browned. Remove from oven to cool. In a small saucepan, bring apricot jam to a boil; spoon over tart. Makes 12 servings.

APPLE STRUDEL

5 large green cooking apples, peeled, cored, and cut into ¼-inch slices
½ cup sugar
1 teaspoon cinnamon
½ teaspoon nutmeg
1½ teaspoons grated lemon peel

½ cup golden seedless raisins
½ pound phyllo dough
¾ cup warm clarified butter
½ cup finely chopped walnuts
¼ cup bread crumbs
Powdered sugar

In a large bowl, combine apples, sugar, cinnamon, nutmeg, lemon peel, and raisins. Brush 6 or 7 sheets of phyllo dough with clarified butter and layer them to form a stack; repeat to form a second stack. Sprinkle nuts and bread crumbs on top of dough in a strip 2½ inches wide; leave 2 inches of exposed dough at each of the narrow ends and about 1 inch along the side closest to you. Distribute apple mixture evenly over nuts and crumbs. Fold each narrow end (2-inch strips) inward; then, starting with the long side nearest you, carefully roll the strudel. Repeat for second strudel. Place strudels 1 inch apart on a baking sheet, seam side down; brush tops with clarified butter. Bake at 400° for 10 minutes, then at 325° for 20 minutes more or until strudels are light brown. Cool for 15 minutes and sprinkle with powdered sugar before cutting. Makes 2 strudels; 12 servings.

Photo opposite
APPLE DESSERTS
Gerald Koser

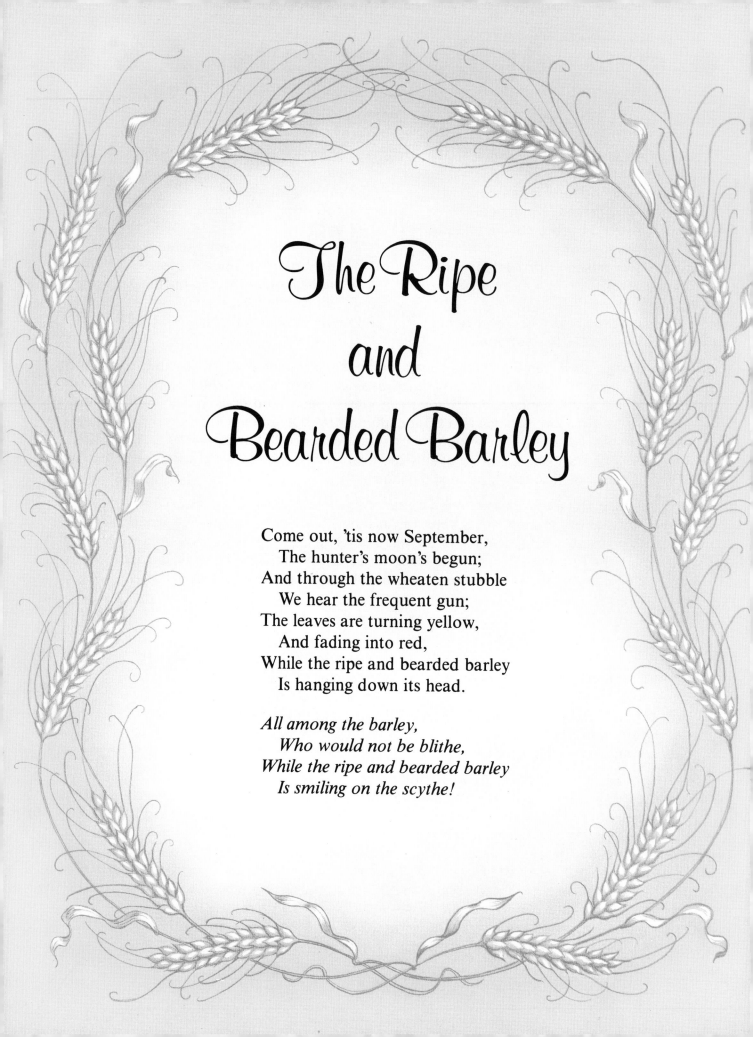

The Ripe
and
Bearded Barley

Come out, 'tis now September,
　The hunter's moon's begun;
And through the wheaten stubble
　We hear the frequent gun;
The leaves are turning yellow,
　And fading into red,
While the ripe and bearded barley
　Is hanging down its head.

All among the barley,
　Who would not be blithe,
While the ripe and bearded barley
　Is smiling on the scythe!

The wheat is like a rich man,
   It's sleek and well-to-do;
The oats are like a pack of girls,
   They're thin and dancing too,
The rye is like a miser,
   Both sulky, lean, and small,
Whilst the ripe and bearded barley
   Is the monarch of them all.

All among the barley,
   Who would not be blithe,
While the ripe and bearded barley
   Is smiling on the scythe!

The spring is like a young maid
   That does not know her mind,
The summer is a tyrant
   Of most ungracious kind;
The autumn is an old friend
   That pleases all he can,
And brings the bearded barley
   To glad the heart of man.

All among the barley,
   Who would not be blithe,
When the ripe and bearded barley
   Is smiling on the scythe!

Anonymous

Autumn Field

High overhead, the mellow sun at noon
Spills gold in payment for a locust's tune.
The faded-yellow cornstalk tents repose
In watchful attitudes, while circling crows

Spread raven wings against an azure sky
To startle field mice with their piercing cry.
Here, too, wild sumac crawls in scarlet stealth
Across brown vines once heavy with a wealth

Of plump blackberries, sweet beyond compare,
That tumbled in ripe confusion everywhere.
Now barren twigs emerge where summer's hand
Once laid a bright green pattern on the land,

And, though the earth is warm, my heart turns cold
With winds that warn me autumn's growing old.

Viney Wilder

Photo opposite
CHICKORY AND OATS
Gene Ahrens

Who Owns Cross Creek?

Who owns Cross Creek? The redbirds, I think, more than I, for they will have their nests even in the face of delinquent mortgages. And after I am dead, who am childless, the human ownership of grove and field and hummock is hypothetical. But a long line of redbirds and whippoorwills and blue-jays and ground doves will descend from the present owners of nests in the orange trees, and their claim will be less subject to dispute than that of any human heirs. Houses are individual and can be owned, like nests, and fought for. But what of the

land? It seems to me that the earth may be borrowed but not bought. It may be used, but not owned. It gives itself in response to love and tending, offers its seasonal flowering and fruiting. But we are tenants and not possessors, lovers and not masters. Cross Creek belongs to the wind and the rain, to the sun and the seasons, to the cosmic secrecy of seed, and beyond all, to time.

Marjorie Kinnan Rawlings

Autumn Witchery

Autumn's magic pattern of
   gold and scarlet flame
Is woven in the woodland
   within an earthy frame.

This fascinating alchemy
   has a sweet, wine-tangy smell
As autumn uses witchery
   to weave her magic spell.

Roy Z. Kemp

Autumn Fire

Ivy burns along the country lane
Where embers glow in every maple tree.
Sparks of sunset, vivid through the boughs,
Touch every shining leaf with brilliancy.
Red oaks flame upon the distant hills
And scorched pastures make a tawny pyre
For black-charred pods of sifted seeds,
As summer is consumed in autumn fire.

Helen Virden

Photo opposite
AUTUMN IVY
Bob Taylor

Nutting

The harvest is nearly over, the fields are deserted, the silence may almost be felt. Except the wintry notes of the redbreast, Nature herself is mute. But how beautiful, how gentle, how harmonious, how rich! The rain has preserved to the herbage all the freshness and verdure of spring, and the world of leaves has lost nothing of its midsummer brightness, and the harebell is on the banks, and the woodbine in the hedges, and the low furze, which the lambs cropped in the spring, has burst again into its golden blossoms.

All is beautiful that the eye can see, perhaps the more beautiful for being shut in with a forestlike closeness. We have no prospect in this labyrinth of lanes, cross-roads, mere cartways, leading to the innumerable little farms into which this part of the parish is divided. Uphill or down, these quiet woody lanes scarcely give us a peep at the world, except when, leaning over a gate, we look into one of the small enclosures, hemmed in with hedgerows, so closely set with growing timber, that the meady openings look almost like a glade in a wood; or when some cottage, planted at a corner of one of the little greens formed by the meeting of these cross-ways, almost startles us by the unexpected sight of the dwellings of men in such solitude.... Even this pretty snug farmhouse on the hill-side, with its front covered with the rich vine, which goes wreathing up to the very top of the clustered chimney, and its sloping orchard full of fruit — even this pretty quiet nest can hardly peep out of its leaves. Ah! they are gathering in the orchard harvest. Look at that young rogue in the old mossy appletree — that great tree, bending with the weight of its golden rennets — see how he pelts his little sister beneath with apples as red and as round as her own cheeks, while she, with her outstretched frock, is trying to catch them, and laughing and offering to pelt again as often as one bobs against her....

Then farther up the orchard, that bold hardy lad, the eldest-born, who has sealed (Heaven knows how!) the tall straight upper branch of that great pear-tree, and is sitting there as securely and as fearlessly, in as much real safety and apparent danger, as a sailor on the top-mast. Now he shakes the tree with a mighty swing that brings down a pelting shower of stony bergamots, which the father gathers rapidly up, whilst the mother can hardly assist for her motherly fear — a fear which only spurs the spirited boy to bolder ventures....

The little spring that has been bubbling under the hedge all along the hill-side, begins, now that we have mounted the eminence and are imperceptibly descending, to deviate into a capricious variety of clear deep pools and channels, so narrow and so choked with weeds that a child might overstep them. ..."Ah, there are still nuts on that bough!" and in an instant my dear companion, active and eager and delighted as a boy, has hooked down with his walkingstick one of the lissome hazel stalks, and cleared it of its tawny clusters, and in another moment he has mounted the bank, and is in the midst of the nuttery, now transferring the spoil from the lower branches into that vast variety of pockets which gentlemen carry about them, now bending the tall tops into the lane, holding them down by main force, so that I might reach them and enjoy the pleasure of collecting some of the plunder myself....

So on we go, scrambling and gathering with all our might and all our glee. Oh, what an enjoyment! All my life long I have had a passion for that sort of seeking which implies finding (the secret, I believe, of the love of field sports, which is in man's mind a natural impulse) — therefore, I love violeting; therefore, when we had a fine garden, I used to love to gather strawberries, and cut asparagus, and, above all, to collect the filberts from the shrubberies, but this hedgerow nutting beats that sport all to nothing.

Mary Russell Mitford

Apple Song

The apples are seasoned
And ripe and sound.
Gently they fall
On the yellow ground.

The apples are stored
In the dusky bin
Where hardly a glimmer
Of light creeps in.

In the firelit, winter
Nights, they'll be
The clear sweet taste
Of a summer tree!

Frances Frost

September

Now mild September hastens to its close;
Some morning, soon, we may expect a frost.
Across the stubble fields a cool wind blows,
And much of summer's loveliness is lost.

But beauty lingers in the garden still,
With hardy mums and marigolds in flower,
And there is music — loud, persistent, shrill,
For insects chirp through every passing hour.

The leaves are clustered thick on every bough,
Though red and yellow mingle with the green.
Intent on migratory journeys now,
In restless, twittering flocks the birds are seen.

In fields where clover yet grows lush and deep,
The woodchucks fatten for their winter sleep.

May Allread Baker

October

October always casts a magic spell
Upon me. I should know, too well,
What nature's autumn wine
Will do to hearts like mine.

My laughing feet will somehow stray
Through dusty leaves. My heart will stay
Beside bright goldenrod
And where pink asters nod.

My steps will pause beside a zinnia bed,
Flaunting heads of orange and of red
With maple leaves, a sheet,
Blanketing their feet.

Melancholy days? Not these!
When nuts fall from the walnut trees,
Must busy squirrels remind me, too,
That I have housecleaning to do?

Alice B. Johnson

A Recipe for Halloween

Take a dozen witches,
  Broomsticks, five or six,
Several hundred goblins,
  Each one up to tricks.

Take some owls a-hooting
  And some scatting cats,
Jack-o'lanterns spooky,
  Several hundred bats.

Season well with laughter
  Harmless fun that's fine;
Add a dish of shivers
  Creeping down the spine.

Stir them all together,
  Looking very sober,
In a big, black caldron,
  Last day of October.

Alice Crowell Hoffman

Sleepy Hollow-een

Washington Irving has written a tale
Of spirits that wander and men who grow pale
On hearing the legends that seem to abound
In quaint Sleepy Hollow near old Tarrytown,

Where once came a schoolteacher down 'long the coast,
Whose lingering time there was shorter than most;
A lean, lanky fellow of loosely hung frame
With small head and huge ears — that's Ichabod Crane.

In fairness to Ichabod, it must be said,
He entered an eerie world faint hearts would dread.
For, in the mind's eye of most Tarrytown folks,
Spirits and spectres were seldom a hoax.

Perhaps the most famous the Hollow had seen
They called "Headless Horseman" — a blackguard, indeed.
He fought with the British in '75;
A cannonball left him no longer alive,

And, now in the evenings, he travels, it's said,
In search of his dignity and of his head.
With a great rush of wind that is heard and then gone,
He tears to the churchyard, his gravesite, ere dawn.

Now Ichabod Crane was the credulous sort
Who believed all he heard, every gruesome report.
His eyes widened awfully in terror, they said,
When told of the horseman out seeking his head.

"The bridge to the church is a bad place to ride,
For that's known as *his* place," one lad did confide.
And, surely, one night, when the hour was late,
Our Ichabod Crane came to tempt his own fate.

Some nights are dark nights, while others just bleak,
And some are forbidding for humans too weak,
But this was the darkest, the bleakest e'er known,
When Ichabod Crane was just starting for home—

Along down the path on Gunpowder, his steed,
Ichabod rode at a sobering speed.
The wind in the branches quite caused him to start.
He whistled then, softly, to quiet his heart.

But, at Wiley's Swamp, a disturbing affair—
A dim, looming figure awaited our pair.
He, too, was on horseback, but answered no word
To Ichabod's "Who are you?" Hadn't he heard?

Well, Ichabod's whistle became a scared song,
And, kicking his horse, he rode frantically on.
Still the dark horseman stayed close on his tail.
Gunpowder panicked and took the wrong trail!

"The bridge to the church is a bad place to ride!"
Good heavens! That's just where our riders had hied!
One glance to the rear and old Ichabod read
That the horseman behind him was hurling a head!

Gunpowder was found next day, grazing content,
But no sign of Ichabod or where he went.
Just the shell of a pumpkin, all splattered around,
Was seen near the churchyard; it littered the ground.

The townsfolk just nodded their wise Hollow heads
And whispered, "The Horseman." Yes, that's what they said.
And those lingering long in that valley so dear
Best take care to believe of it *all* that they hear.

                    Amanda Barrickman

J.BAZZETT

Overleaf
ROCK WALL
Fred Dole

The Gypsy Trail

I must follow the gypsy trail,
   Must be up and away with the dawn!
For I must greet the vigilant sun
   And hear the morning's song.

I must go where the eagle nests
   Atop the mountain peak! —
When you possess a gypsy soul
   The gypsy trail you seek.

I must face the blizzard's rage,
   Must feel its biting cold!
For I was born with a gypsy heart
   And a gypsy heart is bold.

I must rest where the wind's caress
   Is wild as a nomad's kiss!
For I must know what the Great Voice says
   That speaks from life's abyss.

O blessed am I whose gypsy feet
   Are forever doomed to roam,
Companioned by the wind and the stars,
   The whole wide world my home!

Emily Carey Alleman

Gypsying

Anyone can sit in the sun of an early October afternoon when outdoors is at its best and say, "What would I not give to be a gypsy these days, with no responsibility save to roam where nature seemed most beautiful!" Not everyone though would really desire to be a vagabond, with a trust to luck and Providence for food and bed to come at the right time.

In the autumn days when the sham vagabond *talks* of gypsying and its manifest charms, the true gypsy-hearted one is on the road. Nothing but the direst necessity will keep the heart vagabond from the road when September comes.

All normal mankind loves nature outdoors — autumn foliage, hills and rivers, woodland and meadow. Most people love these things in a general, abstract way. The gypsy heart loves winter outdoors well; spring it hails with a poet's joy; summer is a season of luxurious idling, and the autumn is welcomed with a very lover's ardor. Then the foot will not be still; it must out and down the brown highway to the tune of the mellow breezes in the trees, as certainly as the dancer's foot must beat time to the music's rhythm.

When the early twilights fall, with their myriad beauties of rose-streaked sunsets and hillsides of gold and crimson and purple; when the evening comes with a softness of horizon outlines that the other seasons miss, how can one endure four walls? Outdoors is home; indoors, a prison.

But, after all, no one can be told of these things and made a vagabond by any secret rites or occult process. The gypsying joy is instinctive and comes like the poet's inspiration or the artist's temperament. You are a gypsy heart or you are one of the larger proportion who laugh at such enthusiasts. You are as you are. If you cannot understand, be content with the things that Providence meant should content you.

Frank Farrington

The Mist and All

I like the fall,
The mist and all.
I like the night owl's
Lonely call —
And wailing sound
Of wind around.

I like the gray
November day,
And bare, dead boughs
That coldly sway
Against my pane.
I like the rain.

I like to sit
And laugh at it —
And tend
My cozy fire a bit.
I like the fall —
The mist and all.

Dixie Willson

"The Mist and All" by Dixie Willson, from *Child Life Magazine*, copyright 1924, 1952 by Rand McNally & Company. Reprinted by permission of Dana W. Briggs.

Photo opposite
HORNED OWL
Nancy Garlick

Readers' Reflections

Golden Autumn

Golden autumn comes to me
And sings her lilting song:
"Wile away these golden days —
I will not be here long.

"Enjoy, enjoy my sunny days,
My gentle breeze so soft
That loosens downy thistle seeds
And dances them aloft."

Teasing autumn says to me,
"I will try to linger."
Her mellow days, her misty nights
Wrap me around her finger.

Each season brings its special time
And memories for all,
But life on earth seems most serene
When autumn comes to call.

Jo Ann J. Stiefel
Apple River, Illinois

From A Hilltop

Did you ever stand at sunset
On a high and windblown hill,
Beneath your feet, a picture spread —
The mountain, rock, and rill;

The little stream with stepping stones
Like a winding ribbon laid;
The rocky path; the meadow green,
Where grass a carpet made;

The gnarled oak with twisted limbs
So stark against the sky?
It's a pleasant place to dream from
As hazy clouds drift by.

R. M. Mayberry
Fort Pierce, Florida

Autumn's Artwork

There's beauty in an autumn morn,
　Its colours, red and gold.
The sunrise casts a work of art;
　Its secrets yet untold.

There's beauty in an autumn eve
　When sunset shadows fall
Upon the brown and yellow leaves
　Ere winter comes to call.

Helen Roberson
Zion, Illinois

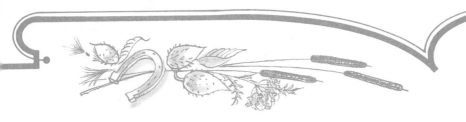

Editor's Note: Readers are invited to submit poetry, short anecdotes, and humorous reflections on life for possible publication in future *Ideals* issues. Please send xeroxed copies only; manuscripts will not be returned. Writers will receive $10 for each published submission. Send material to "Readers' Reflections," P. O. Box 1101, Milwaukee, Wisconsin 53201.

Song of Autumn

Come, take my hand and walk with me
Through the autumn forest;
The trees will all be whispering
Like a phantom chorus.

Hand in hand, we'll see the glow —
A bright, exquisite scene
Of flaming red and burnished gold
Within a sunny beam.

We'll "ooh" and "ahh" in unison.
We'll revel in the sight
And sing the song that autumn brings,
Expressing our delight.

Janet Arnold Lietz
Appleton, Wisconsin

October

What is more enchanting than
    October's autumn treats?
Her trees with ruddy foliage
    transform our humdrum streets.

October's such a gypsy, though,
    her charms we must recall;
For, once she's lost her raiment,
    we have lost our fall.

Edith Tollefsrud
Rockford, Illinois

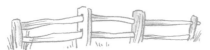

Country Living

When you live out in the country,
    Far from all the city noise,
Your lifestyle is more simple
    And you know an inner joy.

When you live out in the country,
    The birds sing all day long;
They fill the hours with magic
    Through the music of their songs.

When you live out in the country,
    All your neighbors are your friends.
You know a sweet contentment
    That you wish time could extend.

When you live out in the country,
    Nature's there for you to see;
The trees and flowers are certain proof
    Of God's great majesty.

When you live out in the country,
    What with all that you behold,
You *never* would change places
    With another living soul!

LaVon M. Wood
Benton, Louisiana

Alone
With the Fall

The summer people have moved back to town;
  I am alone with the fall.
Grapes in the arbor are hanging down;
  Woodbine is red on the wall.

   Shining horse chestnuts dot the lawn;
     Thorn-apple trees are aglow —
   The summer people have packed up and gone.
     I was glad to see them go.

     The lake and the beach, trees and the sky,
       The late-blooming asters and trailing vine,
     The formal garden, the geese on high —
       With no intruders, the country is mine.

              Bernice Kreitz Abrahamzon

Photo opposite
PICNIC TABLES
Three Lions

I Have Always Said
I Would Go

I have always said I would go sometime in the autumn
　　Away from the bare boughs and the fallen leaves,
Away from the lonely sounds and the faded colors
　　And all the ancient sorrow, and change that grieves.

I have always said I would go — and now it's autumn —
　　To an island where the wild hibiscus grows
And parakeets flock to the groves at twilight
　　And fragrance drifts from bays where moonlight glows.

But there would be the vasty sound of breakers
　　Come in to toss their pearls upon the sand.
All through the night, a longing of great waters
　　Trying to make the vastness understand.

I have always said I would go sometime in the autumn
　　Away from the lonely sounds and change that grieves —
But here in my heart is the sound of a distant ocean,
　　And here in my heart is the sound of these falling leaves.

Glenn Ward Dresbach

When Autumn
Is Upon Us

Snowy, silken milkweed parachutes
Are waiting for the wind to sail and fly;
The leaves of towering maples on the hillside
Flame gold and orange and red against the sky.

Gray squirrels quilting nests with seeds and grasses
Will eat or bury nuts from morn till night;
Certain instinct stirs the feathered masses
And sends them winging on a southward flight.

Man gathers remnants of the garden's giving
And plucks ripe fruit before the coming frost;
He's warned by shorter days and chilly mornings
That yield not garnered now will soon be lost.

So man and plant and bird and furry creature
Prepare themselves against a later hour —
Yet, while the joys of autumn are upon them,
They'll cherish every sunbeam, leaf, and flower.

Virginia Blanck Moore

Season of mists and mellow fruitfulness,
Close bosom-friend of the maturing sun...

John Keats
from *"To Autumn"*

Wanderlust

On a day like this, when the morning's new
And the world seems just created,
My feet have wings, and my whole soul sings
With an urge of time undated.

The road is long and its call is strong,
And my joy stirs deep inside me;
And I want to run and travel on
With only a star to guide me.

The wind's song and the bird's song
And the song of the shining rails,
And the jet's soar and the train's roar
And the breeze in the billowing sails

Say I can't stay, for I must go.
My blood is alive with an aching
For the wide world and the grand world
And the world that is mine for the taking.

Eleanor Chroman

Country Roads

For my own and nature's sake,
I'll take the country roads.
Without concrete, they ride easily on the earth —
Observing all the hills and valleys,
Curving around the woods,
Going, quietly, nowhere in particular.
Little wild things dare to exist alongside,
Scurrying under snowy winter fencerows,
Sipping from spring's wild rosebushes,
Singing on summer's leafy branches,
Sleeping in an autumn meadow of Queen Anne's lace.
Cornstalks, hollyhocks, and brown-eyed Susans
March boldly up to the edge, and
Over by the ditch, elderberries tumble carelessly
Onto carpets of dandelions.
In the fall, when country roads are at their best,
I'll take their slopes of flaming sumac,
Their clusters of bittersweet,
Their hickory nuts and round green hedgeapples,
And I'll listen to the voice of a cricket.

Mary Martin Palma

Abandoned Roads

We are the abandoned roads.
Beside the great highways we linger.
We have faltered, stumbled in the onward march,
And now we look wistfully on.
Resigned, like old people in chimney corners,
We watch these young roads,
Smooth of face, broad-backed, strong-muscled.
How they swagger! How they conquer all obstacles!
"Narrow," they sneer, swerving past us.
Yes, we are narrow. No time had our makers for broad roads.
They must press forward!
But they stirred up our dust with their laughter,
Packed it down with their tears and the sweat of their bodies.
Through the years we have bowed to their burdens.
In their triumphs, defeats, in joyous procession, in mourning,
They have deepened our ruts; they have furrowed our faces.
In silence we watch while the young roads
Lift all care from our shoulders.
Soon our last faint traces will be hidden by grasses and wild
    flowers.
But we have lived abundantly,
We abandoned roads.

Amy May Rogers

Simple Caring

"Why can't you run?" asked the little boy,
   as the old man shuffled along.
"Just pick up your feet; I know that will work."
   He felt he just couldn't be wrong.

"My feet are too heavy," replied the old man.
   "They've been many places, you see,
And have gathered a bit of the cares of the world
   that I can't seem to shake off of me."

"I'll help you get rid of those silly, old cares,
   so they will not stick to your shoes!"
The boy took the hand of the tired, old man, saying,
   "Now you can run, if you choose."

"I don't need to run, son," was the reply,
   and he patted the little boy's hair.
"My feet will feel lighter as I travel on
   because I can see that you care."

With hands clasped together, the two moved along
   in step to the old man's pace.
They said no more, their sharing complete,
   and a smile of content lit each face.

Dawn Corkins

Road Song

Give me the clear blue sky overhead, and the long road to my feet,
And the winds of heaven to winnow me through, and a brother tramp to greet,
With an inn at the end of day for rest, and the world may keep its bays —
For these are the gifts of the wayside gods, and the gifts that I would praise.

Come from the murk of your city streets to the tent of all the world,
When your final word on art is said, and your flag of faith is furled,
When your heart no longer gives a throb at the first faint breath of spring —
Ah, turn your feet to the ribbon-road with a chorus all may sing!

Where the sandalled dawn like a Greek god takes the hurdles of the hills,
And the brooding earth rubs sleepy eyes at the song some lone bird trills,
Where a brook, like a silver scythe of the moon, awaits your warm caress —
Ah, these are the gifts that the high gods fling to mortals in duress!

When the blood-red sun swings low in the west, and an end comes to desire,
When the candle-gloom of the low-ceiled room is bared to a pine log fire,
And the tales of men are told anew till the huntress leaves the sky —
Ah, these are the gifts for the sons of men to set their treasure by!

Then give me the clear blue sky overhead, and the long road to my feet,
And a dog to tell my secrets to, and a brother tramp to meet —
And the years may take their toll of me till I come to the weary West,
And I lodge for good in the world's own inn, a way-worn, waiting guest!

W. G. Tinckom-Fernandez

Photo opposite
AMISH WAGON
Bob Coyle

Autumn Idyll

The laughter of the summer stream is stilled now;
It whispers lonesomely
Beside the woodland path.
Birch and maple scatter tapestries
Where ghosts of Chippewa and Crow roam.
Ash trees flaunt their scarlet fruit,
And from bronzed oaks the acorns fall.
A grosbeak warbles his delight
Atop a Norway pine.
These are the plenteous days,
When heaven hears the harvest songs of earth.
Like purple velvet,
Twilight falls upon the land —
And feathered migrants soar
In arrowed lines across the hunter's moon.

Bess Berry Carr

Tranquillity

To walk a country lane at night,
Beneath the reassuring light
Of moonbeams streaming through the trees,
And recognize beyond all these,
Much farther than the eye can see,
God's pattern of infinity —
To feel the Holy Presence there
Of my Creator's love and care,
And kinship with the nearest star —
I know that Heaven is not far.

Mildred Morris Gilbert

Ideals
Thanks You

In our next issue of Ideals, we celebrate Thanksgiving, and, in the spirit of Thanksgiving, Ideals would like to thank you, our readers and subscribers, for your continuing patronage and your kind letters. Your ideas and suggestions are invaluable to us in selecting inspiring photography, poetry, and prose for each issue.

Our work seems so worthwhile when we receive comments like these: "I would like to tell you how very much I enjoy my subscription to your magazine. Look forward to every issue and savour every page. Really a top notch magazine!" (D. D., Canada) "It's finding Ideals in my mail box that makes such a nice day!" (C. F., Logan, Ohio) "Much appreciation for one of America's most meaningful magazines." (S. S., Sycamore, Illinois) "It (Ideals) has truly been a blessing in my life, as I know it has been in each person's life that has ever had the joy of reading it." (D. J., Carnegie, Oklahoma)

Please, join us next issue in our celebration of thanks, and recall with us those most cherished blessings of family, friendship, and freedom. Remember, too, that a gift subscription to Ideals is a beautiful way to say "thank you" to someone dear to you.

ACKNOWLEDGMENTS

ALONE WITH THE FALL by Bernice Kreitz Abrahamzon from NEW POETRY OUT OF W CONSIN, copyright 1969, Stanton & Lee Publishers; STEP SOFTLY HERE and THE GYP TRAIL from THE GYPSY HEART, copyright 1957 by Emily Carey Alleman; SEPTEMBER May Allread Baker previously published in *Star Weekly;* I HAVE ALWAYS SAID I WOULD C by Glenn Ward Dresbach from ONE THOUSAND BEAUTIFUL THINGS, copyright 1947 by T Spencer Press Inc., reprinted by permission of Patricia S. Daggett; GYPSYING from THE VA ABOND BOOK by Frank Farrington, copyright 1905, published by The Oquaga Press; APP SONG from POOL IN THE MEADOW, copyright 1933 by Frances Frost, reprinted by perm sion of Joan Blackburn; ABANDONED ROADS by Amy May Rogers from THE DESK DRAW ANTHOLOGY, copyright 1937 by Doubleday, Doran, & Company, Inc.; ROAD SONG by W. Tinckom-Fernandez from ONE THOUSAND BEAUTIFUL THINGS, copyright 1947 by T Spencer Press Inc.; OLD CHURCH BELL from SONGS OF THE PRAIRIE, copyright 1965 Stella Craft Tremble, Prairie Press Publishers; THE OLE RAIL FENCE from THE OLE RA FENCE AND OTHER POEMS, copyright 1939 by Ray Whyte, McDaniel Press Publishe AUTUMN FIELD from A TRIBUTE TO EDUCATION by Viney Wilder, published by Warp Pu lishing Company. Our sincere thanks to the following authors whose addresses we we unable to locate: George Hugh Baldus for ROADS TO TOWN; Bess Berry Carr for AUTUM IDYLL; Kunigunde Duncan for OCTOBER SONG from her book PRAIRIE SONG, copyright 1968 by Branden Press Inc.; Mildred Morris Gilbert for TRANQUILLITY; Alice Crowell Hoffm for A RECIPE FOR HALLOWEEN from HEIGH-HO FOR HALLOWEEN, copyright 1948 by El abeth Hough Sechrist, Macrae Smith Publishers; Bertha R. Hudelson for THE REASON FO AUTUMN; Alice B. Johnson for OCTOBER from her book WHERE CHILDREN LIVE; and Myr Van Campen for THE LEISURE ROAD.